Snails

Snails

Peter Murray

THE CHILD'S WORLD®, INC.

Library of Congress Cataloging-in-Publication Data
Murray, Peter, 1952 Sept. 29-
Snails/by Peter Murray.
p. cm.
Includes index.
Summary: Introduces the physical characteristics,
behavior, and life cycle of snails.
ISBN 1-56766-382-6 (alk. paper)
1. Snails—Juvenile literature. [1. Snails.] I. Title.
QL430.4.M89 1997
594'.3—dc21   97-1044
CIP
AC

Photo Credits

COMSTOCK/COMSTOCK, Inc.: 16
COMSTOCK/John Cooke: 19
COMSTOCK/Russ Kinne: 23
COMSTOCK/Townshend P. Dickinson: 9, 29
DPA/DEMBINSKY PHOTO ASSOC: 15
Doug Locke/DEMBINSKY PHOTO ASSOC: 6
Jim Roetzel/DEMBINSKY PHOTO ASSOC: 24
Joe McDonald: cover, 10
Richard Shiell/DEMBINSKY PHOTO ASSOC: 20
Robert & Linda Mitchell: 13
Sharksong/M Kazmers//DEMBINSKY PHOTO ASSOC: 26
Stan Osolinksi/DEMBINSKY PHOTO ASSOC: 30
Stuart Westmorland/Tony Stone Images: 2

On the cover...

Front cover: A land snail explores the ground
Page 2: This underwater snail has a brightly colored shell.

Table of Contents

No matter where you are, there are snails living close to you. Look for them in the middle of the night. Or early in the morning, when the dew is still on the grass. Or after a gentle spring rain. Those are the best times to find snails.

Snails do not like bright sunlight. They do not like freezing temperatures. And they do not like hot, dry weather. Snails like cool, shady, moist places. Look for them under logs, old boards, or in piles of dead leaves. If you look hard enough, you will find a snail.

This snail is crawling on a rock.

What Do Snails Look Like?

Some snails have flat, coiled shells. Others have pointed shells that look like cones. A snail's shell always grows in a spiral, and it has one large opening. The snail can push most of its body out of the opening, but it never leaves its shell. A snail's shell is part of its body.

Land snails can be as tiny as the head of a pin, or as big as a plum. In some parts of the world, they grow even bigger. One snail, the *Giant African land snail*, weighs two pounds and has a pointed shell that is almost 11 inches long. That's about the size of a football!

This snail has a beautiful spiral on its shell.

The snail's spiral shell protects its soft body. It keeps the snail from drying out. And when a snail is in danger, it pulls in its **tentacles**, or sensors, and hides in its hard shell. But what's inside the shell?

A snail's body isn't like yours. You have bones and lots of organs that help you live. All that is inside a snail's body are its heart, its brain, and its digestive system. Snails also have a tiny breathing pore under the lip of the shell. It leads to the snail's **lungs**. The lungs help land snails breathe air, just like you!

A snail's body is soft and moist.

When a snail is active, most of its body is outside the shell. You can see it's slimy body and its tentacles. If you look closer, you can see the snails eyes. Snails have bad eyesight. If you stand very still, it probably can't see you.

The snail's mouth is a small opening under the front of its body. Inside the mouth is the radula. The **radula** is like a tongue with lots of tiny teeth on it. When the snail eats, it uses the radula like a file. It grinds the food into bits so it is easier to swallow.

This *garden snail* has most of its body out of its shell.

How Do Snails Move?

People have two feet. Cats and dogs have four. Insects have six feet. But snails only have one "foot." Snails are members of the **gastropod** family. Gastropod means "stomach foot." A snail's "foot" is really its belly. Slugs are gastropods, too.

To move around, snails need to make their own "highways." Just behind the snail's mouth, a gland makes slippery, slimy **mucus**. That is what the snail slides around on! The snail's foot ripples like a wave. It moves the snail slowly along the slimy highway.

Snails like this one use their slimy "foot" to get around.

Most land snails eat plants. They like tender young shoots and fresh green leaves. They also eat flowers, fruit, roots, and vegetables. Even mushrooms taste good to a hungry snail.

Some types of snails eat rotting leaves or dead animals. This helps the dead things decompose and turn into soil. And sometimes snails use their raspy radula to grind away bits of rock or bone. This gives them calcium to help them build strong shells.

This snail is eating a leaf.

Where Do Snails Go In Dry Weather?

When the weather is hot and dry, snails withdraw into their shells and seal off the opening with mucus. The mucus dries to a hard, protective plug. All the moisture in the snail's body is kept inside. Only a tiny pinhole stays open so the snail can breathe.

While the snail waits for rain, its heartbeat and all its other body functions slow down. This is called **estivation**. The snail might stay sealed inside its shell for a day or two, or for several months. When it senses moisture, the snail will break the mucus seal and crawl off in search of food.

This *Florida tree snail* has sealed itself inside its shell.

Where Do Baby Snails Come From?

During warm, wet spring nights, snails perform a courtship dance. They crawl in circles around each other. They touch each other and press their bodies together. Snails are **hermaphrodites**. That means that each snail has both male and female body parts. When snails mate, they exchange sperm with each other. The sperm **fertilizes** the eggs hidden inside both of the snails' bodies. Once the eggs are fertilized, the baby snails inside begin to grow.

A week or two later, each snail lays its own eggs. Some snails dig a hole for their eggs. Others lay them under rocks or dead leaves. A common garden snail lays up to 50 eggs the size of a BB.

Two snails mate on the forest floor.

In a few weeks, the baby snails begin to break out of their tiny eggs. They look like their parents, only smaller. The shells of baby snails are so small and thin, you can see light through them!

The babies start to eat right away. Their first meal is their eggshell. Then they go looking for a tender leaf. The more the baby snails eat, the faster they grow. As the snail grows, its shell grows around in a spiral. If you look at the middle of the swirl in an adult snail's shell, you can still see the shell it had as a baby.

This snail and its eggs are attached to a weed.

Land snails have relatives in oceans, lakes, and rivers. Pond snails live in fresh water. They have lungs, like land snails, and must come to the surface to breathe air. Sea snails breathe with **gills**, like fish.

Sea snails come in many shapes and sizes. Many of the most beautiful seashells—periwinkles, whelks, conchs, and cowries—are the shells of sea snails. Some of these snails eat seaweed. Others feed on shellfish and other sea creatures.

These *Red Turban snails* are covered with algae.

Do Snails Have Any Relatives?

Take a close look at a garden slug. This little creature is a lot like a snail. It has tentacles like a snail's. It crawls along on a trail of its own slime, just like a snail. It eats leaves and shoots, and likes moisture—just like a snail!

Even though slugs and snails are a lot alike, they are not the same. There is one big difference. Snails have shells and slugs do not. When a snail gets too dry, it pulls into its shell. Slugs must crawl under a rock or find some other moist place to hide.

Slugs like this one are close relatives of snails.

Are Snails In Danger?

Lizards, beetles, crows, frogs, and many other creatures eat snails. The *snail kite* is a bird that eats nothing but tree snails. It uses its hooked beak to tear the snail from its shell. Another animal that only eats snails is the firefly larva. It injects a poison into the snail. The poison kills the snail and softens its body. Then the larva can crawl into the snail's shell and eat it.

People eat snails, too. Large snails are raised on farms in France. Snails that are raised for food are called *escargot* (es–kar–GOH). Escargot are served in fancy restaurants all over the world.

This *snail kite* is getting ready to hunt for snails.

People are one of snails' biggest enemies. They kill land snails with poison and pesticides. They kill sea snails for their beautiful shells. Some sea snails have become very rare. Now, laws keep people from taking them from the ocean.

People also kill snails accidentally. Snails are very sensitive to air and soil pollution. By keeping our planet clean, we can make it a better place for snails—and for people—to live.

This snail is attached to a tree.

Glossary

estivation (ESS–tuh–vay–shun)
Estivation is when an animal's heartbeat and all its other body functions slow down. Snails go into estivation when they are waiting for wet weather.

fertilize (FUR–tuh–lize)
Snails fertilize the eggs that are inside each other's bodies. Once the eggs are fertilized, the baby snails inside begin to grow.

gastropod (GAS–truh–pod)
Gastropods are animals that move by using their bellies like feet. Snails and slugs are gastropods.

gills (GILZ)
Gills are what many underwater animals use to breathe. Sea snails and fish have gills.

hermaphrodite (her–MA–fruh–dite)
When an animal is a hermaphrodite, it has both male and female body parts. Snails are hermaphrodites.

lungs (LUNGZ)
Lungs are air sacks that many animals use to breathe. Land snails have lungs, and so do you.

mucus (MYOO–kuss)
Mucus is the slippery, slimy stuff that snails use to move around. Snail make mucus in their bodies.

radula (RA–juh–luh)
A snail's radula is like a tongue with lots of tiny teeth on it. When the snail eats, it uses the radula to grind the food into tiny bits.

tentacles (TEN–tih–kuls)
Tentacles are the sensors on top of a snail's head. When a snail senses danger, it pulls its tentacles inside its shell.

Index